Coffee Conversations

The Simple Leadership Secret of High Performance Workplaces

—◆◇◆—

A Story Book for Managers and Leaders
by Shane Garland and Grant Donovan PhD

—◆◇◆—

Featuring stories from the iconic Australian companies, Qantas and Woolworths

Copyright © 2012 Grant Donovan PhD, Shane Garland

All rights reserved.

ISBN-10: 1477573399

EAN-13: 9781477573396

Coffee Conversations

The Simple Leadership Secret of High Performance Workplaces

Foreword

Dexter Dunphy AM
Emeritus Professor
University of Technology Sydney

Recently, I was looking over the retrofitted headquarters of a large Australian corporation. Walking around with the senior executive responsible for the retrofit, I observed how innovative the design was and how well everyone seemed to be working – there was an enthusiastic conversation going on in a cluster around a table in the kitchen; there were clients being interviewed in attractive glass 'pods' with views, there were individuals deeply absorbed while working alone at workstations. I had known my guide for years and I remarked: "Rosemary, you have done it again!" For in the past I had seen her coordinate the creation of other high performance workplaces where people became deeply engaged and committed to their work. She smiled and responded: "Dexter, you and I know how simple it is. You just ask people what they need to get their work done and then you make sure that happens."

What a revolutionary idea! That we treat every member of the organisation, from CEO to cleaner, with respect. That we recognise they are usually the greatest experts on how to do a good job where they work – if they are given a chance to contribute.

In "Coffee Conversations" Shane and Grant take the reader through a series of stories exploring this deceptively simple notion that organisational greatness and high performance emerge from initiating a respectful dialogue that has the power to transform the life of organisations.

I often wonder why it took me years of studying and working with organisations to reach the simple conclusion; that the life of organisations resides in the ongoing flow of conversations that take place between those in the organisation and other stakeholders outside who deal with the organisation. In these conversations, which can occur face-to-face, on telephone, email or Facebook, people create the culture of the organisation, that is, their notion of what the organisation is about, what it means for them to be in the organisation and how to go about their work. So if we want to change an organisation, we have to change what people talk about and, because the multitude of voices are theirs, that is close to an impossible task unless they themselves decide to change the meanings conveyed in this ongoing stream of communications. Those in an organisation made the culture, they own it and, if it is to change, they are the ones who must change it.

An important part of the content of organisational conversations are the stories which are generated as people discuss critical incidents, retell their versions of what happened and give the events meaning. In many organisations, these stories convey disillusionment and cynicism, the inevitability of failure, the uselessness of really becoming committed to performance. These stories often become embodied in what I refer to as 'rogue rituals' – repetitive conversations around the water cooler or elsewhere that reinforce sub-optimal behaviour: "Don't waste your bloody time volunteering for that project. It's just another talkfest!" You can hear the hollow echoes of past conflicts in these conversations; voices from the interpersonal underworld that keeps everyone locked into apparently safe but ultimately self-defeating, deadening patterns of behaviour that cripple organisational performance.

As change agents, if we are to work with those in an organisation to create a different future, we must plunge into the hot human process where it matters most – where the day-to-day work gets done. And working to define a vision of a compelling new future that people can identify with, despite their fear and cynicism, is central to the change process.

In this short and very readable book, Shane and Grant share with us how they have achieved this in the organisations where they have worked. This is not a theoretical discussion but rather an absorbing account of how they actually made transformational change in some important organisations; how that change transformed people's lives, creating a new level of engagement in their work, and also how it produced impressive bottom line results. This is not a work of fantasy because I have been a witness to some of this as it happened. So read the book; reflect on what you can take from it to inform your own practice as a manager or change agent; but most importantly put these ideas into action yourself.

Grant: Getting the Conversation Started

Most people hate work. They only do it for the money.

Now, it is true that some people love what they do and would continue to do it without pay but that group makes up only a tiny percentage of the workforce. Stop paying the rest and they would leave so fast, you wouldn't see them for dust.

Most people like their managers but hate being managed. They hate bureaucracy and the lack of freedom to be involved in the decisions that affect their work.

We know this because what people like and hate about work has been extensively researched, so there are no secrets surrounding the differences between high performing worksites and the poor performers. The high performers treat people well and engage them in the decision making while the poor performers treat people like a commodity.

These differences between organisations can easily be seen in their language and stories. The differences are rarely in their resources and equipment. Sometimes, it may be in their business models but, more often than not, it's in the way they treat their staff.

More specifically, the difference is in how well staff and managers converse with each other. How often they sit down for coffee and have quality, two-way conversations, with every conversation building on millions of previous conversations to ultimately create an organisation's performance story - its culture.

Every organisation has a story; a cultural narrative that describes how the organisation began, how it has been managed, what it values and how it is likely to perform in the future. Every organisation also has a language; a set of words, acronyms and conversation patterns that drive the behavioural interactions and culture.

It is also true that every individual has a personal story and this, in part, is our story.

A story of how Shane and I serendipitously met in 1994, when Shane was Perth Airport Manager for Qantas and I was hosting a presentation on high performance worksites by the Saturn Car Corporation.

Shane arrived at the session, with 10 of his staff, keen to explore the secrets of a high performance workplace. He listened carefully, asked some good questions then left. A few days later, he invited me for a drink to discuss the Saturn story further.

This coffee conversation was the beginning of our joint but separate journeys. We have been in constant contact over the past 18 years and, except for a period in the late 1990's where we collaborated extensively when Shane was the General Manager for Qantas at Sydney airport, we have followed two very different journeys; Shane as a corporate manager at Qantas and Woolworths and myself, as a corporate coach and researcher, in a variety of organisations and in a number of different countries.

At every Coffee Conversation along the way we have discussed our personal observations about workplaces and have reinforced the same, blatantly obvious conclusions - treat people well and they will perform well, treat them badly and all the consultants, coaches and leadership programs in the world won't help.

This is our story about high performance leadership and best practice management. A continuous narrative of observations and practical experiences that explore the very simple secrets of working with staff to get the best possible outcomes for everyone, including all employees, their managers, their organisations and their customers.

Most people don't like going to work. They would rather be doing something else; something active, something challenging, something engaging. It's not that they don't want to work; they just want choice, variety and ownership over what they do.

People need stimulation and an opportunity to think. An invitation to participate in the decisions that affect their working lives. What they don't need is little or no freedom and some arbitrary person, called "the manager," giving orders.

Taking orders is rarely motivating for most people but giving orders is normal practice in most families, schools and workplaces.

Technically competent but socially challenged, many managers have little or no idea how to really engage their staff or how to have the basic conversations that lead to excellent performance outcomes. They are not silly people but many do not seem to possess the ability to have simple, engaging, empowering conversations with their staff.

Shane and I have written this book to help leaders and managers explore the simple art of Coffee Conversations. An art, once mastered, is guaranteed to deliver exceptional performance outcomes.

The book is a collection of practical stories from Shane's experiences inside Qantas and Woolworths, two iconic Australian companies, while I have added supporting thoughts, observations and data gathered from my own experiences working with both Shane and a large variety of organisations scattered throughout the world.

We hope reading this book stimulates you to pick up your phone and invite some of your front line staff to coffee.

Don't email them or text them or ask your PA to arrange the meeting. You start the conversation and when you finally sit down to a drink ask them this question……What do you think we are doing well as an organisation and what do you think we could do better?

The rest will take care of itself.

Shane: Too Many Chiefs and Not Enough Indians

When I was first starting out in my working life, I interviewed for a casual position with QANTAS for a three-month temporary position at the very entry level of the organisation. The position included meeting incoming aircraft and assisting passengers getting off the aircraft at Melbourne Airport. It also included assisting passengers requiring wheelchairs to get to and from the aircraft. That's about the sum total of the job.

The funny thing was, at that very first interview, I decided I wanted the job of the guy who was interviewing me. He was the Customer Services Manager (CSM) of Melbourne Airport and, blow me down, ten years later I was appointed to the position. That job was all I wanted and I got there. Airport Manager and General Manager roles came later.

The three or four years prior to my appointment as Melbourne CSM, I was working interstate and overseas for Qantas, so had missed some of the new structural developments being pushed by upper level management.

One development was the introduction of teams and team leaders into airport operations across all airports. Just before my appointment to the Melbourne CSM position, the company had advertised for 20 plus new Team Leaders in Customer Service and had already conducted interviews and appointed the successful applicants. When I arrived, the entire Customer Service department and the unions were in an uproar over the hiring process because upper management never consulted anyone and they all felt left out.

At the heart of the matter was confusion about "what does a team leader do?" The department already had far too many levels of management without squeezing another level in. The current structure was worker, supervisor, superintendent, department head, duty manager and airport manager. All this management for 120 people and now we were adding more than 20 new team leader positions.

The company's view around structure was always about control and supervision. It was never about allowing people to do anything on their own; to be empowered. Delegation of authority was slim and staff always needed to check with a supervisor before they could make a decision.

Over my first few weeks we started to sort out new rosters, people issues, job descriptions and began readying everyone for the roll out of the new structure. We had just grown the Customer Service department from 12 supervisors and managers to a workplace with approximately 32 supervisors and managers for 120 workers. So with senior management expectations of improved service and lower costs they were in for a shock.

Talk about how to piss off all your staff with one big expensive head office initiative. All of a sudden we had an army of team leaders and supervisors roaming around the airport bossing around frontline workers, dictating what they could and could not do. This took months and months to sort out.

Frontline staff were complaining, team leaders and supervisors were always bitching about who was doing what and how hard things were. Managers tended to find pleasure in highlighting problems and everyone was blaming everyone else. Really, it was a negative "we know best" culture, with plenty of "that's how it's always been done."

It was difficult for me to lead a positive conversation because this was the department that had inducted me earlier and, as the new leader, I was part of the problem. The culture was very closed to new ideas and the general view was that "management has stuffed it up again."

My overriding thought was "surely coming to work should not be this negative or such an unpleasant experience for everyone."

I am not certain where the idea came from but after months of turmoil somebody suggested that "maybe we should have a look at how other companies ran their operations?"

The joy of a positive suggestion coming forward was something for me to grab. It was exciting to be working on something that would open us up to new possibilities, so not really knowing what value or upside there would be I just needed to give it a go.

We organised to run an exchange program for 16 staff to visit and work in four other companies for one week and in return, we would host 16 people from these same companies into our business. We drew up a program as interesting as we could, trying to inspire the other companies to do the same. We exchanged staff with the Ford Motor company, Telstra, Australia Post, and the National Australia Bank.

My boss at the time thought I was wasting time and openly said he did not understand the point of the exercise - "what do you hope to achieve Shane, these companies aren't even airlines?" I tried to explain that we needed to open the place up to what's possible. I didn't really know or care what our staff would come back with; I just wanted them to look outside our four walls.

I know I thought the opportunity for personal development was important. I also thought how they briefed management and staff on their return was equally important. The nitty gritty detail of how the other companies worked was not important. The mere fact that 16 people had the opportunity to look outside our very closed world of work was unbelievably important.

The positive energy that was created by this initiative seemed to be infectious. For months after the visits staff would bring up little things they saw or learnt from the other workplaces. It would come up in general conversations or in meetings, with more and more people coming forward with "what if" scenarios. They were not always spectacular ideas but small positive thoughts instead of the constant negative mutterings. It was a good experience for everyone.

As it turned out, the staff were really impressed with the way the Ford Motor company had approached the team leader concept. It was different to our approach; it was very much a people approach, a caring approach, with a very supportive style. It actually changed the basis of how we introduced the Team Leader initiative. I also think it highlighted how we missed the whole idea that it was not about organising ourselves into teams, it was all about developing better teamwork to ensure our customers received better service.

This was very early in my management career and the whole exercise taught me how destructive it can be to add more management and supervision layers. My experience then and since has been to lift performance you really need to make sure that you have great leadership capability in all staff, not an excess of supervisors and managers running around, making it tough on the people doing the work.

Fewer chiefs and more engaged Indians at the frontline of customer service is critical.

Grant: Evidence Supporting Engaged Cultures

I did not meet Shane until he arrived in Perth a number of years later but it was obvious then that his Melbourne experience had shaped his ideas around the need to build great customer service through engaged and empowered teamwork.

Shane had not read any of the empowerment books but he knew intuitively what was being written in management research around the world at the time; that engaged, flexible and empowered work cultures easily outperform traditional, manager centred bureaucracies. The evidence is spread throughout the research literature and was the over-riding observation on all the best practice management tours I led around Australia, the US and Europe throughout the 1990's.

One of the best studies generating supporting evidence was written up in *Corporate Culture and Performance*, a 1992 publication by John Kotter and James Heskett from Harvard, who conducted an 11-year study of corporate cultures across the US between 1980 and 1990. They reviewed the results for 207 large US companies in 22 different industries and found that Adaptive Culture Companies (ACC), those that are flexible, have great teamwork and work to satisfy the expectations of their customers, employees and stockholders always perform better than Strong Corporate Cultures (SCC), which are more traditionally focused, with rigid hierarchies.

Their research figures show the ACC's experienced average revenue increases over the study period of 682% versus 166% for the SCC companies. Other performance differences included share price increases of 901% versus 74%, growth in staff numbers of 282% versus 36% and, most importantly, average profit increases of 756% for the ACC's versus 1% for the SCC's.

Jim Collins in *Good to Great*, Barry Macy at Texas Tech University, the people at Great Places to Work and a whole host of others have gathered extensive research evidence supporting engaged and empowered workforces as the best performers.

Probably one of the most frequently cited studies is Daniel R. Denison's research of 34 large American firms where he found that companies with a participative culture reap an ROI that averages nearly twice as high as those in firms with less participative cultures.

Many companies complain that their employees are de-motivated, unproductive, and disloyal. Jeffrey Pfeffer, a business professor from Stanford University, argues that these companies get exactly what they deserve. If you create a toxic or dysfunctional work environment then you're going to get those types of behaviours from your workforce. According to Pfeffer's research, companies that engage and empower their staff will outperform companies that don't by 30% to 40%.

Pfeffer also found that over the 20 years from 1972 to 1992, the US companies Wal-Mart and Southwest Airlines had respective share price rises of 19,807% and 21,775%. Yet during this time, their industry competitors performed very poorly as a group. What these two extremely successful companies have in common is that their sustained advantage did not rely on technology, patents or strategic position but rather on how they managed their workforce.

Again, without labouring the point, all the evidence is conclusive; treat people well, engage them in running the business and the performance will follow, just as Shane finds every time he works with a new group.

Shane: Learning the Power of Coffee Conversations

Airport manager Adelaide was my first general management position. All my experience and training up till this point had been in customer service or in the technical side of airport operations; how to check in customers, balance aircraft for weight distribution, order fuel and load baggage and cargo. So, my knowledge or concept of a full management role was limited, except for my personal observation that much of what managers did was mostly control people in a very unpleasant way, with little respect or caring.

I wasn't a trained manager but here I was in a nice new office, in my nice new suit, with an in-tray and an out-tray. Not much went on in that office.

After observing the operation for a few days, I waited for all the aircraft to depart one morning then I sat down in the general staff office and began chatting over a cup of coffee with Peter, the supervisor. Peter appeared to be the backbone of the operation. He had been there a very long time and knew everything but I noticed over the first few days that he often appeared frustrated.

We had just begun our first conversation when he grumbled, "So when will you be moving the photocopy machine?"

I had no idea what he was talking about so I asked him why he thought I would want to move the photocopy machine. He said, "That's what all the new managers do. As soon as they arrive they move the copy machine from the operations room to just outside their office for their own convenience."

As nothing much was going on in my office, I had very little need for a copy machine, so I assured him that it could stay where it was. Even today, I'm still baffled as to why new managers, and old managers for that matter, want to keep changing things around and causing operational hurdles for people who actually do the frontline work. But it happens.

I found Peter to be a source of great knowledge and help, he was sitting on a mountain of information about how things worked and a major part of his frustration was being surrounded by non-performance issues and not being able to address them. How frustrating must that have been to see a real need for change yet management's first priority was to rearrange the office.

My coffee conversations with Peter are probably where my management style was accidentally born. It was where I realised that a social chat over a cup of coffee could generally solve most problems.

So I began having more regular coffee conversations after aircraft departed. In one conversation, I asked Peter what else he thought we could do better.

He replied quickly with, "So why does Qantas pay more for everything than any other airline?"

I was a little stunned but Peter had been such a reliable source on everything else that there must have been something in what he was saying, so I asked him to give me an example. He gave me three.

He firstly showed me how Qantas was being skinned alive with rental charges by the Federal Airports Corporation. We were getting done badly and there had been no company response other than to increase budget accordingly each year.

Second, he showed how Qantas was paying for all airplane waste to be disposed of as expensive quarantine waste when only the waste from international flights needed quarantine treatment. The resulting changes in waste disposal practices produced huge cost savings.

Thirdly, Peter asked why Qantas was paying more for crew accommodation than any other airline in Adelaide. I still remember my feeling of 'this can't be true.' We were the biggest airline operator in town and we took more hotel rooms than anyone else. We were the big fish in a small pond; surely we were getting the best deal?

I wasn't sure where to start, so I rang the Qantas contracts department in head office but did not get a warm reception. They gave me the brush off, saying they had the most professional and most astute general managers organising contracts and it really was not my issue. They said they would get back to me.

About two weeks later I received a letter from the contracts department thanking me for my inquiry and advising me there were three criteria determining the room rate. One was the overall relationship with the hotel, secondly, the time of the year the contract was written and thirdly, the industrial situation with crew at the time.

Suddenly, I knew what it was like to be Peter; management not listening, being stone walled at every turn and fed rubbish.

Not to be deterred, I made an appointment with the Director of Sales at the Hilton Hotel in Adelaide for the following week. I was not quite sure what I would say at the meeting but I was definitely motivated to show Peter we could change things together. Our relationship was building, he trusted information with me and I needed to demonstrate actions, not words.

I remember feeling quite nervous on my way to the hotel meeting. I had not done this before and was well aware I was stepping outside the boundaries of my position.

I was warmly welcomed by the sales director and we made small talk about Adelaide and general business. It was all very polite but I was looking for a way to broach the main issue. Sensing by his body language that my time in his office was coming to an end I waited for a pause in the conversation and softly told him that I was aware we were paying more for accommodation at his hotel than any other airline and that he should be aware that the other hotels in Adelaide were being very competitive right now.

His response was immediate. He put his hands behind his head, lent back in his chair and asked, "So how much would you like to be paying?" He had me; I wasn't planning on an immediate capitulation. I had to think quickly. I knew the other airlines were paying about 15% less than we were, so I said I would like to pay one dollar less than anyone else. I'm sure that wasn't the smartest response but it was all I could think of at the time. He agreed to my request on the spot.

I felt elated but, as a very new manager, I still had the dilemma of how to explain my actions to the guys in head office. So I suggested to the sales director that it would be better if the change was seen as his idea. He agreed and I was relieved to be out of his office and heading back to the airport.

Back at the airport, my relationship with Peter and other staff went from strength to strength.

Adelaide was my first management role and it was where I learned that listening to people who actually do the work, valuing their inputs and creating an environment where they feel comfortable putting forward their ideas is fundamental to good people management and is empowering for the individual.

It is where I learnt the power of the coffee conversation.

Grant: Taking a Risk

Over the years I have worked with hundreds of middle and upper level managers across a range of industries and just like Shane, the very best have always been calculated risk takers. People who will put actions to their words and take on stupidity wherever it lurks. The not so good performers tend to hide behind company policies and procedures and never do what's right. They just do what they're told.

This lack of confidence in a manager is crippling to the people they manage. A manager's role at any level is to be bold and to lead. Not to hide behind the bureaucracy. Employees hate weak managers who say one thing and do another. Managers who won't listen and won't act to support their staff.

Employees want managers who are prepared to lead from the front and remove all the stupid bureaucracy that prevents staff from achieving great outcomes. People come to work each day wanting to do their best but poor leadership makes it too difficult and employees just give up. Good leaders take risks.

Shane: A Picture Tells a Thousand Stories

I moved on to become Qantas Airport Manager in Perth at a time when Qantas and Australian Airlines were merging. The brief from our CEO was to merge operations where possible and get the best available performance outcome. It was believed we could achieve good financial and operational benefits from merging the two operations.

As normal when two groups merge, their cultures were obviously different and both believed they had the "right" culture, so divisions and emotions ran high. I will leave it to others to discuss the difference between the two cultures but I felt Australian Airlines brought a breath of fresh air and an attitude of what was possible. It was a very exciting time and one of my first tasks was to merge the Ramp Operations of both airlines; baggage handling, aircraft cleaning and other 'under the aircraft' support functions.

Early on in the process, the new ramp manager, Alan, suggested how this could be done, with the resulting performance and financial benefits flowing through. His proposed changes looked good on paper but would it be possible to bring two blue collar, heavily unionised and industrial action prone groups together?

This was something that had never been done at any airport in Australia, so it was a challenge worth giving a go.

We organised the normal round of meetings with staff, conducted briefings, presented financial models and all the usual stuff management do but our staff and the unions weren't convinced. So more and more meetings were called, with the only outcome being that everyone, managers, frontline staff and the unions, were exhausted by the process. The traditional way of negotiating was delivering the traditional response and getting us nowhere.

Whenever we gathered, always in the same meeting room, the behaviour consistently slipped into aggression and a "change is not possible" attitude. Every time it felt like both sides were putting on their war paint and getting ready for battle.

Little progress was being made until we moved some of the discussion outside of the room. At one meeting, John O'Connor or JJ as he was known, the state secretary of the powerful Transport Workers Union of Australia (TWU), was present. The staff strongly supported JJ and they trusted him much more than they trusted Qantas management.

The meeting had been going for a while and, as usual, we were getting nowhere. So, I asked the group if they would mind if I took JJ for a walk around to show him our new facilities. John agreed and if it was all right by him it was all right by the group. So, off we went for a walk. John was a legend in the industry and I was a little nervous about taking this giant of a man for a walk but I thought a private conversation outside the room might help.

We started at the check-in side of the terminal and made our way around the various work areas, finishing in ramp operations.

At the check in counters, I had the opportunity to point out that all the Australian Airlines check-in counters had been removed and replaced with Qantas branded counters. As we moved through the terminal he could see the Australian Airlines signage at the departure gates had also been replaced with Qantas signage. We then walked through the ramp lunchroom where he could hear discussions taking place among staff about the merging of the rosters. We finally moved out onto the tarmac area where he could see the signage at the top of the new Perth terminal had also been changed from Australian Airlines to Qantas.

I could see all this was having an impact on him and completely unplanned, we turned around to see a 737 aircraft taxiing into the new terminal. I explained that only last week the aircraft had been painted in Australian Airlines colours but now it was painted in the Qantas livery. Neither of us had to say anything more.

As we wandered back into the terminal to resume our meeting with the others, I shared my thoughts with John that the merging of these two workforces was causing stress to all staff and that I didn't like people being stressed when working with heavy equipment as it dramatically increased their risk of an accident. I said we were compelled by economics to make the changes and that his help would go a long way to minimising the stress on staff and that I would appreciate his help.

Not much else was said between us.

As we went back into the meeting room, with the union delegates and ramp management present, I was still not sure what would happen next. To my relief, JJ put his hands on the contentious rosters in the middle of the table, moved them forward to the delegates and said quietly but firmly "boys, we will be working these new rosters from the 15th of next month. No fuss, no, hoo-ha. Just a general let's get on with it."

I will never know who was more stunned the delegates, the other managers or me. From that moment on, my respect for and working relationship with JJ was solid. It also gave me confidence to continually find new ways of communicating with the unions and everyone for that matter.

Grant: Everyone a Business Partner

What Shane has always done well is not argue his point but immerse those around him in the economic realities of the business.

Over many years as a corporate coach and researcher, reviewing all manner of strategic plans, interventions and training programs, I have seen nothing work better in aiding performance improvements than building the business acumen of every employee.

Every worker and manager needs to understand explicitly that sooner or later, in a global economy, many uncontrollable economic and political forces will threaten their jobs. Witness the recent economic meltdowns in Europe and the US.

What we know with certainty is the fortunes of all economies and businesses will continue to rise and fall. We can't always predict when they will rise or fall but we know they will continue to cycle up and down and, while individual companies and their staff have no control over world economic forces, they do have enormous control over how they respond.

For example, some of the best performing companies we know have flexible reward systems where everyone takes a share of profit when the company is doing well and everyone takes a pay cut when the company is doing poorly. They are flexible and able to ride the waves.

The common problem with existing award and enterprise agreement pay systems is that workers lose at every turn. When the economy is booming and businesses are doing well, workers rarely share in the increased profits. When the economy performs poorly, efficiencies are demanded and workers begin losing their jobs in bouts of rightsizing and redundancies.

The best reward systems allow for everyone to share equally in the profitable times and for everyone to take a cut when times are bad. True empowerment means the elimination of any legal controls over the labour-capital relationship.

Tenure and desired remuneration can never be guaranteed. Great organisational performance is the only possible protection for people who either choose to or are forced, by economic circumstances, into working for an employer. Either way, individuals have to take responsibility for their own performance. Everyone is their own business.

Quite simply, customers pay all salaries and wages. If customers don't buy your products or services, you don't have a job. Contrary to popular belief, workers and managers are not paid by their organisations and unions have absolutely no way of guaranteeing employment. Customers have control. Even government departments who fail to service their customers (taxpayers) will eventually disappear.

Empowered, business literate work teams have evolved for good business reasons. They are at the frontline, closest to the customer and, if given the decision making power, can ensure every customer feels special.

Hierarchies and bureaucracies, with decision making at the top, unshared financial information and lots of control and command systems (like performance appraisals) can't possibly respond fast enough to truly elate a customer.

Hierarchies are a corruption of purpose because managers too often become the staff member's main customer. As Shane has always inherently known, the manager's main customer is the frontline worker. Managers are there to provide all the resources, education and freedom workers need to service every customer at the highest possible level.

Filling in requisition forms, performance appraisals and any other action designed to meet management's need for control adds cost to products or services without adding speed or quality of response for the customer.

The Game of Business is mostly a very simple competition between organisations offering similar goods and services to a finite customer group. The Customers they are all competing for want the highest quality product or service, at the lowest possible price, when they want it. If they can't get it from your organisation then they will go somewhere else, taking their money and your job with them.

To win the competition, staff must produce the highest quality product or service at the lowest possible cost and if the teams produce outstanding products or services, the organisation can ask a premium price.

The support team, including executives, operational managers, supervisors, accountants, human resource officers, technical specialists and others watching the game, are there to help and resource staff to produce their very best performance. End of game!

As Robert Heller writes in *The Super Chiefs*, "The record breaking best seller, In Search of Excellence (Tom Peters and Robert Waterman), was a recipe of comfort for the CEO. It enshrined the existing order. It looked mostly inward (only one of the eight attributes of excellence, 'continued contact with customers,' a fairly mealy-mouthed formula, looked outward). It affirmed that you, the chief executive, could centrally command corporate success......... No wonder so many of the Excellence companies flopped."

Central control of business illiterate staff is a recipe for poor performance. In our experience, the best available education tool to help staff develop their business acumen is *Zodiak: The Game of Business Finance and Strategy,* which is part of the Paradigm Learning stable of excellent business simulations. Shane used Zodiak to help a number of frontline Qantas staff at Sydney Airport to become more business literate.

Shane: Burning Baggage Handlers

After Perth, I became the 17th Qantas General Manager at Sydney Airport in 25 years and I had walked into a toxic environment full of industrial action and dysfunctional, angry behaviours.

Sydney was a very political, heavily unionised work site, with poor work practices, terrible customer service, shocking relationships all round and a very high cost operation. The Qantas executives at the time believed if they could get the management model right at Sydney airport then they could roll it around to all Australian airports and end up with a great airports operation.

It was a split decision between the Qantas executives at the time about my appointment. Fortunately for me, the real decision got down to the CEO, James Strong, who was and remains a great supporter.

I was responsible for all operations, including all arrivals and departures, the customer service agents, the Qantas Clubs and all the baggage handlers who were known then as the 'inland Wharfies'.

The baggage handlers had been treated very badly by management for a very long time and the battle lines had been drawn years before, with strong-arm tactics on both sides being the name of the game. It was a common occurrence to end up in the industrial relations commission to resolve the simplest of disputes between management and a hostile workforce of about 1000 people. The baggage handlers were treated as the bottom rung of the organisation and it was trench warfare. Often with the frontline workforce sabotaging the operation days before management even knew about it.

One of the old chestnuts the TWU (Transport Workers Union of Australia) would pull out to upset management, knowing management had been unable to resolve the problem for more than 20 years, was the issue of wet weather gear; raincoats.

For years they had worn bright yellow plastic gear that didn't fit, got very sweaty, had a protective barrier that was broken down by jet fuel and when rain poured off aircraft, it would run down their necks and sleeves.

The year before I arrived, management were so fed up with this issue they purchased, at extreme expense, the great Australian Drizabone raincoat for every individual. Only to find out they were completely inappropriate.

So here I was, with the same wet weather gear problem, in a typical negotiating room; union delegates down one side of the table and management on the other, with nowhere to go because management and the company had never been able to find a suitable rain protection product.

I did not want to get into promising something and then not delivering, so I was determined to make the staff and the union part of the solution, not just identifiers of the problem.

I was honest and told them that I didn't think the company nor I could solve the issue, so I proposed they form a group, identify what was needed, design the wet weather gear, identify the best material, source it and have it made. It would be their choice.

You should have seen the looks on their faces. The union delegate who could get most fired up just stared. He said, "You're kidding aren't you?" I said no, you wear it not me, I think all the effort that has gone before us produced nothing, so how about you guys take ownership and see what you can do.

He said, "You will trust us to do that?"

I said, "Yes."

The group wanted more info. For the very first time they were interested in how much things cost. It was agreed they should look for the best wet-weather gear at or below what we were presently spending on rain protection gear. Every one left the meeting scratching their heads. At least we weren't fighting.

Whilst the group were off searching, costing, getting more groups involved, we discovered Qantas was spending $50,000 a year on replacement wet weather gear because the baggage handlers hated the current gear so much, some of them would throw it in the rubbish bin when they came in from loading an aircraft and then get a new set next time it rained. It was tragic.

In just a few meetings the baggage handlers showed great progress. They took ownership, they were proud and they demonstrated a good business sense around costs. All was going well, so well, we made an agreement that the new gear should be signed for by the individual and not replaced for two years.

I could not be more pleased, we had ownership happening and for the first time, some respect for company property and most importantly, a semblance of trust was beginning to develop.

We signed off on the deal for the new gear, under budget, with no replacements available for two years and everyone was happy.

A few days later I received a request from the Qantas Director of Airports to meet in his office, where he presented me with a letter intended for the CEO, from the General Manager of Uniforms.

As you can imagine, the letter attacked everyone; Sydney airport management generally, me specifically, the baggage handlers and the unions. Apparently I had been irresponsible, Sydney airport was out of control, the baggage handlers had taken over and chaos was everywhere.

The GM for Uniforms put a value of 30% above our purchase price, claimed it was the "Rolls Royce model for wet weather gear" and it did not meet Qantas standards and could possibly burn and catch fire. Her letter was purposely constructed to crush whatever we were doing as quickly as she could. The letter had a desperate air of losing control.

The director asked me for my side of the story and my first verbal response was to say that "I've never seen a baggage handler burn in the rain."

I explained all the details of the situation and he, along with the CEO, supported me. It could have very easily gone the other way. The director and CEO trusted me, they supported me and they created a space in the organisation where I could work.

Of course, there were two good lessons in the raincoat saga. Firstly, staff can manage themselves, within budget and secondly, no manager can succeed in changing work practices without senior leadership support.

Without that support the bigger culture will get you.

The baggage handlers purchased the right gear; we saved hundreds of thousands of dollars and for the first time demonstrated the value of trust and engaging staff in running the business.

Grant: The Self-Employed Worker

Shane's response to the chaos and opposition he found at Sydney airport was to involve staff in running the business.

Probably the greatest shift I've witnessed over the last thirty years has been the evolution from employees just attending work to staff becoming responsible business partners, with a central focus on the costs of running the business. No individual today can afford to waste money with poor work practices or they may find their job at risk.

This simple fact is demonstrated in a number of high performing organisations by the multiplier conversation, which goes a little like this; "There are 1,000 people working here and if everyone wastes 10 cents each day, through one poor work practice, then $31,300 is wasted each year on that one practice and that is $31,300 we don't have to pay for the extra resources and people we need."

So every individual needs to become a business person and treat their workplace like it was their personal business.

Cliff Hakim's book, *We Are All Self Employed*, proposes that the global economy has created a new "social contract" where every person has become self-employed. He suggests the need to see ourselves as self-employed has arisen because organisations themselves have lost any semblance of stability and certainty.

Hakim argues that organisations will be continually forming and reforming and that people must "move from the role of dependent employee, ever-adapting to survive, to independent-interdependent worker, ever creating to succeed."

He also predicts that very few people will survive the empowering changes of the future without the mindset of a self-employed individual.

Shane: The Trust Factor

It was probably about six months after I started at Sydney airport that things started quieting down a little. The industrial stoppages had ceased and mutual respect was growing. The conversation had changed and staff were beginning to enjoy being listened to in a genuine way.

It was definitely a new experience for the baggage handlers whose only view of a large organisation was their long experience at Sydney Airport. Some of them had been working there for 20 and 30 years. They were long-term workers who had been exposed to nothing but fights with management and many honestly thought that this was how it was at every worksite.

Around this time, Grant was taking one of his study groups to the US to visit some really high performing work sites. It was agreed by all the managers that sending some of our staff would be a good idea. There wasn't much point just sending the managers as the workers would have viewed it as a junket and little interest would have been shown in management's thoughts on their return. So we sent a group of frontline workers, including a union delegate and one manager from each area.

There was a lot of talk and fuss within the organisation at the time about not trusting these guys to do the right thing and how poorly they might behave while they were away. Not trusting the staff ever entered my head. If we were ever going to make a real leap forward then they needed to see for themselves what was possible.

We needed to send very loud and very positive signals that change was possible.

On their return from Grant's study tour a large group met to hear their experiences and to gauge if it was worthwhile. I had no idea how this meeting would go.

I was amazed at what came forward. One manager, Peter Breuer, said he now saw Sydney airport as "runners up" and that he wanted Sydney airport to be the best run airport or business in the world.

Then each person took it in turns to talk about all the positive ideas they had seen and what we could try at Sydney airport to turn this non-performing, high cost work site around.

The biggest impact of the trip, however, was on the union delegate, Ross Lewis. Ross came back energised to support change and to transform the work site into a positive environment for all the people he represented.

The study group had even drawn up a plan of what they would like to change and suggested we start with small steps. The group shared their ideas with other groups of workers and it was mostly received well, with very little resistance, except for a few disbelievers who still doubted management would let the workers get involved.

The frustration for the group was how to brief every worker on site, considering there were 1000 workers. The study group and the union were adamant that if we were to be successful then every person needed to be briefed and included in the plan for change.

So great was their energy, their enthusiasm, their business plan and their vision that we agreed, if it would help to get us started, to include everyone.

The question was, how do you brief 1000 people? Answer, we invited them all to dinner on the same night but more about the dinner later.

If you think getting people involved in sourcing raincoats got the tongues wagging in head office, you can only imagine the rumbles going on when they heard we were sending frontline workers on a best practice tour and then throwing them dinner so they could tell their mates.

Grant: Motivating Staff

What Shane achieved by sending the group overseas was to motivate a large group to do better. Even those who did not travel were energised by the stories their peers told and by the knowledge that Shane was a different type of manager; a manager who listened and was keen to help staff learn and grow.

I would like a dollar for every time a manager has asked me for help to motivate their staff.

My answer is always the same, "your staff are already motivated. They don't need motivating. They just need you, as their manager, to set an environment where they can all be engaged." And that's what Shane does naturally.

Like schoolteachers and parents, most managers think of staff as children who need either a carrot or a stick to perform. Nothing could be further from the truth. Kids have a natural desire to learn, to find out about the world around them and to participate with others as an equal.

Adults are the same, they love to learn, to grow and develop their knowledge and talents. They want to be good at what they do, regardless of whether they are labouring away in a mine or conducting open-heart surgery.

People are intrinsically motivated to do well but most organisations place so many policy and procedure barriers in their way that all discretionary effort is sapped and staff end up doing the bare minimum; keeping an eye on the clock, ready to leave at the first opportunity.

Alfie Kohn explains human motivation well in his book, *Punished by Rewards*, where he describes how both external carrots and sticks, as ways of manipulating human behaviour, destroy personal motivation. He cites many studies that show all punishment is destructive and all external reward systems create long-term damage, especially when the task is already intrinsically motivating. That's why in our work at Perception Mapping we find so many professional people, like engineers in construction companies and doctors in hospitals, so disenchanted and demotivated. They love their work but are weighed down by the reward and punishment manipulation.

Kohn cites over 70 studies showing extrinsic motivators, like praise and more money, are not merely ineffective over the long term but counterproductive. Other studies show that when people are offered a reward for doing a task that involves a degree of problem solving or creativity or just for doing it well, they will tend to do lower quality work than those offered no reward and are operating on the purely intrinsic motivators of fun and engagement. The authors of the bestselling book *Influencer: The Power to Change Anything* call intrinsic motivation the first and most powerful source of energy.

Shane taps that energy every time he creates the environment where staff can solve their own problems.

Shane: Time to Save Money

We had been on our journey of turning around our performance at Sydney airport for about eight months and things had really changed. It was peaceful, I could go for a walk around the terminal and staff would stop and talk about the business. They wanted to tell me what they thought we could do differently to get a better outcome.

I have always found that staff initiating business conversations is a very good sign that performance improvements and substantial cost savings are not too far away. You could feel we were starting to gain momentum and our costs had stopped increasing. The next step was to start bringing them down.

Many people believe in major change initiatives that costs usually go up at first before they come down. I have never subscribed to that view. It may happen if you go about it the wrong way or go for the big bang approach but never if you base the change on coffee conversations.

I really believe if you implement the change at a pace staff can cope with, all will be good. I much prefer to get 1000 people thinking and implementing performance improvements rather than half a dozen managers thinking they own all the best ideas.

At about this eight-month point I was having a coffee with Ross Lewis, the senior union delegate, and Ross calmly said to me "well everything seems to be going well around here, how long do you think it will last?" This was a defining moment. Ross, without explicitly saying so, was enjoying our new way of working. There was lots of good two-way communication, staff were getting all the performance information they needed and a sense of ownership, involvement and respect was developing. Everyone was feeling better about how we were operating and it was a lot less stressful for everyone.

I thought about Ross' question and was straight and honest with my response. I told Ross that I liked the changes so far and that I enjoyed how we were working. I then went on to say that I appreciated his question and that I thought we would probably have 12 months to demonstrate a real financial turnaround or one or two things would happen to derail our journey or direction.

I said 12 months because, from my experience in the organisation, they would not tolerate the lack of improvement or major turnaround in the business outside that time frame, as evident from 17 airport general managers in 25 years. I also knew that even though I had incredible support from my director and the CEO, we had to be delivering major cost savings in the first year or that support would start to wane.

At a personal level, I had to balance this time pressure, with my conviction that until you get the environment right not much positive is going to happen.

So I told Ross that one of two things would happen if we were not able to deliver a better financial performance; either the organisation would change the leader of Sydney Airport (me) or they would bring in a Boston Consulting type group to advise the organisation on what to do.

I let Ross know that I was prepared to stick with the strategy of engaging staff in the change challenge but the timeline needed to be reasonable or the opportunity for everyone would be lost. Ross and I both agreed that we didn't like the idea of someone else coming in and telling us what to do, as we had both been burnt by that approach before.

My memory of how this coffee conversation ended was nothing more than a nodding acceptance by both of us that it was time for a serious attack on costs and that we would get every staff member involved. This was the defining conversation. The point where we were about to demonstrate to the organisation what was possible and, on reflection, I know I felt excited as we walked away.

I announced only days after the coffee with Ross that the international ramp operation needed to save $5 million dollars off its manpower (salary and wages). That was 10 percent off the $50 million a year currently being spent and this would only be the beginning of many cost saving initiatives to follow.

As always, the communication strategy was to include everyone. So we organised a very large meeting of all key stakeholders, both the formal and informal leaders. This meeting was directional at first; I set the scene and advised that the organisations requirement was a $5 million reduction in manpower costs. I then turned the meeting into a conversation about how we could get there. I must say a lot of coffee conversation work went on behind the scenes, with the movers and shakers, to make sure we had a high level of support within the room.

This meeting was mostly scene setting but it was amazing how quickly people bought into the idea that they should get involved and that maybe, taking manpower costs out might contribute to a better working environment for everyone. Most staff knew where the money was being wasted and many were already pissed that nothing was being done.

We agreed on a series of local issues that staff would work on in their own areas and we set two target dates. The first, four weeks from the initial meeting was to begin actions that could deliver half the cost savings, with the remaining actions being delivered in the following four weeks. We knew we would make mistakes and we would need recovery time but, most importantly, we set ourselves up for success not failure. We agreed to reconvene in two weeks to show where the cost saving would come from.

Most pleasing to me was that management and frontline workers had come together for the first time to work on a substantial business issue with the same aim and it was all possible because Ross had asked a critical question over coffee.

Grant: No One Likes a Poor Performer

While Shane and Ross were building their relationship and attacking the cost issues head on, I was running a series of conversations around the country for workers from all manner of organisations to share their experiences. We called these three-hour conversations, Team Clusters, where organisations would send between five and ten frontline team members to converse with workers from other industries.

These were literally coffee conversations between 50 to 100 people, including some of Shane's staff from Sydney Airport.

The Clusters ran in five cities for six years, four or five times a year, and were extremely successful in helping many organisations develop a different conversation between management and workers.

More importantly, all the conversations were recorded and the notes were written up in small books that were given to everyone who attended one or more sessions.

I often read back over those books, looking for patterns in the conversations that can help in the development of questions for the Perception Mapping diagnostic surveys we conduct for organisations around the world. And there have been two strongly recurring themes - work team members hate working with poor performers and they hate managers who don't do what they say they will do.

I say hate because these two behaviours set off an extremely strong emotional response.

The reality is, most people go to work each day wanting to do their best only to be stymied by poor management, demotivated co-workers and low performance cultural systems. In truth, they come motivated to increase revenues and reduce costs and, as Shane found at Sydney Airport, many frontline workers hate seeing poor performance and waste when they know things can be done much better.

Shane: Owning the KPI's

Two weeks after announcing the need to save 10 percent off our manpower costs at Sydney airport, we brought the group together to present their ideas and strategies on how this was to happen.

They had done a lot of work and we knew they were ready to show what was possible. There were fifty or sixty frontline workers and their managers in the same room, with the same vision and determined to be successful. The whole process was inspiring for everyone and I can only hint at the joy it gave me.

It gave me enormous pleasure walking into a room full of people that were excited about their presentations, seeing them having their ideas listed, implementation strategies planned and the costs graphed on spread sheets down to the last dollar. I remember thinking this is good, this is very good.

One group after another, proudly standing there, taking ownership, implementing change, saving money. With all the detail required and without any need to negotiate with unions or management.

Something else happened at this meeting that was defining. They were determined to be successful and wanted to ensure all front-line workers would know if they were achieving their target on a daily basis?

Unbeknown to me, they had already sat down with the financial manager at Sydney airport and devised the simplest of KPI tools. Each group would calculate how many hours they each used to turn an aircraft around. Multiply the number of hours by the manpower hourly rate and then divide this by the number of aircraft each group handled in the day. This was an incredibly basic KPI tool but it worked. No fancy spread sheet just a simple tool. Most importantly it was their tool, they owned it.

You would be surprised at what effort the corporate naysayers went to in trying to prove that this was a poor KPI that lacked any science. But I didn't care how simple it was, it belonged to the staff doing the work and it worked.

The short story here is that the costs came down, everyone hit their targets and we were well on our way to lowering costs even further, improving customer service and turning around our safety performance.

Grant: Meaningful Measurement

Everyone needs a scoreboard. Part of performing well is receiving constant feedback about your performance, with 'constant' being the operative word. Continuous feedback allows a performer to make running adjustments, to make small, continuous, quality improvements.

Measures that enable minute-to-minute performance improvements deliver best performance outcomes.

Groups we took to visit the Fedex operation in Memphis were always struck by the number of scoreboards employed around the operation to ensure everyone knew how many packages needed sorting and how long it was taking, with deadlines for getting planes back in the air and the packages to customers across the US, on time.

Every high performance site we've ever visited has very simple, visual KPI's that everyone understands and can personally impact.

I always remember hearing Ricardo Semler, the author of *Maverick* and part-time CEO of the famous Brazilian company, Semco, reiterate many times that performance measures should always be "few but meaningful."

Unfortunately, too many organisations we visit have KPI's that are many and meaningless.

Shane: The Famous EBA's

I cannot think of anything that tests the relationships you have built with staff and the unions more than going through the Australian Enterprise Bargaining Agreement (EBA) process.

The whole basis of EBA's requires workers and unions to come together and "negotiate in good faith" but if you don't have a good relationship and you don't trust one another, how can you ever come up with a meaningful, mutual agreement, let alone an agreement that supports a good performance outcome. The fact is you can't because the disruptive process of "he said, she said" begins and once you start name-calling, it's just impossible to recover.

On the other hand, if you have put in the time, had the coffee conversations, built great relationships and you trust one another, you can do amazing things. The best example of this at Sydney airport happened when even greater efficiencies were required and the Qantas executive had decided to put many jobs on the line with a competitive tendering process. This meant staff that had been doing the work for a very long time would only keep their jobs if they could demonstrate new efficiencies. If not, contractors, who could do the work for a much lower cost, would be hired.

In normal circumstances, such a threat would generate immediate and significant industrial action but the staff and the unions accepted going down this path because for 18 months we had talked in every conversation about the need to be competitive and everyone knew they could do better. They seemed to relish the challenge and they knew their job security was in their hands.

Every coffee conversation over the previous 18 months had contained some essence of a business conversation, with the question, if this were your business, what would you do differently? For 18 months they had demonstrated they could do great work, so rather than being antagonistic to the process of competitive tendering, staff excitedly took up the challenge.

Their first step was to undertake a complete review of all jobs performed by each area before bringing the total operation together in one tender document. The internal Qantas team then put their tender bid up for evaluation against external bids from companies around the world such as Jardines from Hong Kong, Ogdens from America and Brambles from Australia.

To my delight, everyone went about the challenge with gusto, with a real determination to win, to be competitive and to own their jobs on the merit of efficiency, not by right. They honestly believed they knew how to load planes faster and better than anyone else in the world and showed they had the skills, enthusiasm, discretionary effort, innovation and knowledge to beat the competition.

All that negative energy and pent up frustration from arguing with previous management went into a competitive spirit and aggression focused on beating the competitors on an international scale.

The details and intricacies of how our people put their bid together is another story but the short story is that dramatic and important changes were implemented with lightning speed.

The baggage handlers, ramp and customer staff won the tender as judged by a high powered corporate consulting group employed by Qantas to validate and asses each bid on its merits. The result was cost savings of over $50 million dollars across Australian airports. This was a harmonious period, with no industrial disputes arising throughout this process or for years to follow.

The outcome was really unbelievable and it still amazes me the results that can be achieved when you engage staff in the challenge. I remember every coffee conversation through that period was charged with positive energy about the possibilities. I can't remember one where staff were negative about the company for putting their jobs at risk.

Grant: Engagement Takes Time

When I'm watching Shane conversing with staff and slowly building his relationships, I am also watching his staff and their reactions to his style. Some love engaging immediately while others take time to come around, if ever.

Shane's coffee conversation style requires patience and persistence. It takes time to listen and get to understand each person's motivations and preferred working styles. It takes time for Shane to gain the confidence and trust of each person, and to help each person overcome their personal fears around potential changes to their working life.

Over the years, I have worked with many organisations where staff resistance to change has slowed or completely stymied the best laid plans for performance improvement. The relationships between managers and their staff seem to fracture easily as personalities clash and completely different views of work make an aligned outcome difficult to achieve.

Many people find it hard to break away from their comfort patterns and simply fear change itself. This is where the metaphorical coffee conversations come into their own, to help allay the fears and energise people with possibilities because everyone sees the world differently over a relaxed cup of coffee. The relaxed brain is engaged and sees endless possibilities while the stressed or fearful brain goes into defensive shutdown.

Shane: Fixing a 30 Year Old Problem

One of the issues that came up regularly in our coffee conversations at Sydney Airport was the number of injuries happening to staff loading wide body aircraft.

To make more money, airlines take the space not used by passenger baggage and add cargo and mail. The introduction of wide body aircraft allowed the pre-loading of bags, cargo and mail into containers and cut down turnaround times by up to 50 percent but there was one big problem.

The in-hold systems in these aircraft were a combination of ball mats in doorways and drive wheels that drive the units forward or backwards. When they worked they were brilliant because only one operator was needed to load a hold. However, when not operating properly, they required workers to push and pull containers and pallets weighing up to 4000 kilos. All this while standing on an aircraft floor made up of ribs that were a few centimetres wide and 600mm apart and workers at all airports sustained injuries by falling between the ribs.

Some would lose skin from their ankles to their knees but the worst injuries were spinal. The height in the holds was 1600 mm, which required most workers to bend over and push or pull very heavy units compressing their spinal cords. The workers compensation bills at Sydney were horrendous and the LTIFR hovered around 150. We injured a worker every day!

A team consisting of workers, leading hands and the manager, Peter Breuer, were asked to investigate the issue and recommend how to fix what was really an airplane design problem.

The team found the roller balls on the mats were placed in the wrong position and would not "pick up" the weight of units. They also discovered that damaged roller balls could not be replaced without taking the whole mat out, which could only be done during a major maintenance check. Further, the roller balls in 747 aircraft were inferior and could only handle units up to 2 tonne and the drive systems used easily worn rubber wheels that could only be changed once a year.

The investigation team recommended that all floors should be filled in and the balls on the roller beds be upgraded and put in the correct positions. They also suggested that damaged balls should be easily replaced, tyres be put in the correct position and regularly pumped, and that Power Drive Units should be replaceable within five minutes.

The Senior Engineering Manager was invited to hear the ideas but was not very helpful to say the least. A project engineer turned up at the next meeting and the difference was amazing. A different person, with a very a positive attitude and everything was possible.

To cut a long story short, we formed a dedicated team and the recommended changes went all the way to the aircraft manufacturer, Boeing, where they were incorporated into all new aircraft.

The outcomes of the teams work included all 747 floors being filled in, all ball mats replaced with heavier duty balls in the right places and all new aircraft having upgraded power drive units. At Sydney, these changes, plus other initiatives led to a reduction in lost time injuries from 150 to six and helped improve on time performance for aircraft departures from the low 80 percent level to high 90s.

If the resulting financial gain was important you can only imagine how these people felt about being part of fixing a 30-year-old problem. The whole exercise was unbelievable from beginning to end. Saving millions and millions of dollars but most importantly, saving staff from injury.

The benefits were felt by loading and unloading staff right around the world and all because staff at Sydney airport were encouraged to put their thoughts forward over a friendly cup of coffee. I found out years later that James Strong was also working quietly in the background, with the manufacturer, to help us succeed.

Grant: A Tale of Two Airlines

Of course, the obvious question from Shane's experience with the in-hold system damaging so many workers is why didn't the company do something about the problem earlier? Why weren't they out there trying to save people from injury and reducing their operational costs at the same time because when it comes to high risk, highly competitive industries, nothing beats commercial airlines. Even small economic downturns hurt them badly and if they make a mistake, everybody dies.

Thankfully, there are two airlines out there with great safety records, Southwest and Qantas. However, safety alone does not equate to high performance business outcomes. You also need a good business model, effective business strategies, great systems and, above all, a dedicated and motivated staff to execute. This is where the stories of the two airlines separate.

Qantas is an Australian domestic and international carrier that began life more than 90 years ago, became a government enterprise in 1947 and was fully privatised as a public company in the mid-nineties.

Southwest Airlines is a US domestic carrier that began life in the early seventies after prevailing in a Texas Supreme Court fight against larger airlines that feared new competition and tried everything to stop Southwest flying.

Both airlines are unionised, have around 30,000 staff and carry the largest number of passengers in their respective countries. Southwest has been profitable for all but a couple of financial quarters throughout its history and is promoted by the most prestigious business schools around the world as a high performance case study. Qantas has been up and down.

If you invested $10,000 in each company when they listed, your investment in Southwest is now worth millions, while your Qantas investment is now worth thousands. Southwest has delivered a consistent quarterly dividend and 11 stock splits. Qantas has had some good years and some not so good years.

Southwest are recognised for their fun, people based culture, while Qantas is often in conflict with its workforce. At Southwest, managers are encouraged to "do their people work first and their paper work second." They hire fun staff that really like serving customers. For them, it's staff first and customers second. They treat their staff well and their staff treat the customers well.

Anyone who has flown Qantas knows they have a different story. Some of their staff are great but some just don't like customers. More importantly, their current and immediate past management seem to have a running conflict with staff. A conflict that spills over to the customer's flying experience.

Both companies have different narratives, different memetic patterns. Southwest was born with a warrior spirit, taking the competition head on, with a group of employees who would do anything to help the company be successful. The Qantas story is one of bureaucracy and entitlement that only time in government ownership can really create.

Southwest are not perfect but they do love their people and they celebrate their performance at every opportunity. Their first President and CEO, Herb Kelleher, loves a party and established a very strong team culture from the beginning. Qantas have been at war with their staff over the last decade and, according to my experience with Shane, have only ever had anything approaching a Southwest feel when James Strong was CEO and Shane was General Manager at Sydney Airport between 1996 and 2001.

Shane had a keen sense of timing and like Herb, loved a party. Whenever he saw the opportunity to engage staff and reward performance improvements, he would pounce. Sometimes the celebrations would be over a coffee, with one worker. At other times, they would be large, all in affairs.

Sometimes, his celebrations happened before the performance.

Shane: Celebrating Early

After we had all agreed on how we wanted to change and operate Sydney Airport, it was not a hard decision to brief every worker and to get their buy-in.

I must admit, inviting 1000 people to a sit down dinner in the grand ballroom at the Sydney Airport Hilton Hotel, was another matter. But we were sitting on the opportunity of a life time, the workforce wanted to talk about how they could change, improve themselves and the company, which was a long distance from them being on the grass and costing millions of dollars with disruptions and lost customers.

So, we took a giant leap of faith, sent out 1000 invitations for dinner, took a deep breath and waited to see what would happen. The first reaction was from the work force, "Is it true, have management really invited us to dinner?" The second reaction was from head office, "Is it true, have management really invited them to dinner?"

The response was fantastic, with 600 people accepting the invitation. Those who couldn't make the dinner were either on annual leave or working that night, so we arranged separate briefings later for those that could not attend.

As the dinner drew near, I realised just how big and how important the night was going to be, so I invited the CEO, James Strong, along to see us in action.

The night finally arrived and I will never forget being in the foyer of the Hilton Hotel, welcoming 600 staff and feeling their sense of excitement. No one could predict how the night would go and just as the ballroom was filled, James and his wife, Jeanne-Claude, arrived. I'm sure I was thinking "what have I done here" and "will we be able to control this group." Talk about being on a knifes edge.

Everyone had dressed for the night, nice shirts and ties. This was their night!

When James and Jeanne-Claude entered the ballroom, the seated crowd went into a riot, everyone jumped to their feet, they were clapping, cheering loudly, the level of excitement was unbelievable, the place was out of control.

I doubt if any CEO has received such a rapturous welcome by their staff. I was wondering if we would ever get the dinner back to order. But sure enough when James and Jeanne-Claude took their seats, everyone else respectfully took theirs and Grant, who was MC for the night, got the show on the road.

We started with the staff presentations before eating and everyone listened quietly. They intently took in the information and it was very well received.

The group that travelled overseas had developed presentations on what they had seen and how they thought the whole Sydney operation could change. A few workers who did not go on the trip also presented short presentations on their own improvement ideas to show that not all good ideas came from outside. The final presentation was left to the union delegate, who did a magnificent job and I was left with just a small wrap up at the end before James was given an opportunity to respond to what he had heard.

During the presentations, Jimmy Mitropolus, a really big burly Greek guy said to the crowd, looking straight at our CEO, "When I come to work I feel like I have to leave my brain in the car park. I don't want to do that, I want to come to work and use my brain as well as my body."

When James Strong began his response to the group he started by addressing Jimmy and suggesting, "that's why the car park is always too full." It was a classic comment that showed he understood exactly what everyone had been saying through the night and that he wanted them to be involved in running the business with their ideas as much as their muscle.

Everyone had a laugh but the seriousness was not lost on anyone. What company, or CEO for that matter, wants people feeling like they have to leave their brains in the car park?

James went on to talk about how important it was for this group to be doing what it was doing. He told them he appreciated their efforts and how he looked forward to watching their progress and he subsequently found a lot of time to encourage and support the staff at Sydney Airport. We were off and running!

For months, I thought about that excitement in the room when James and Jeanne-Claude entered. The baggage handlers were bathing in recognition, recognition that they existed, that they were important enough to be invited to dinner and the CEO was there for them. They were celebrating respect and recognition.

For the next few years James would often call into the airport to see how we were doing and he was always warmly received.

Somehow, that night at the Hilton had signalled a real change. It wasn't long before we were operating at 27.5 % lower unit cost and still having fun.

A reasonable question at this point would be, "was the intervention of a best practice tour with Grant (considering air flights were free) and a solid communication evening that included dinner for 600 staff appropriate and worthwhile?"

The answer is obviously yes, it was a great investment. Our savings from no industrial disputes, people coming to work interested (saving on lost time) and the beginnings of an improved safety performance had more than covered any costs and with the real savings still to follow. The early celebration and expense was only in proportion to the opportunity.

Grant: Great Places to Work

What Shane and his team were doing at Sydney was creating a great place to work. A place to have fun, to be involved and to be challenged to run the business better than anyone else could.

What Shane was doing, without reference to workplace writers like John Naisbitt, Tom Peters, Joel Barker, Rollin Glaser, Charles Manz and many others at the time who had researched and written extensively on the characteristics of the best performing companies of their era, was to intuitively develop a great place to work.

Combined, these writers suggested a great organisation is a place where people want to come to work because it is fun, includes real participation in the decision making processes, provides challenging work options and offers good financial rewards. It also provides a pleasant working environment, encourages humour and play, promotes risk taking, strongly values personal excellence, promotes self-management and has company leaders who exhibit positive attitudes and behaviours.

Recent surveys of Australian workers suggest that approximately 80 percent of people "don't like going to work." When asked why, they nominate the absence of the previously mentioned characteristics as the main reasons.

Shane: Discretionary Effort and the Bottom Line

I have no idea of how you measure discretionary effort. But I do know, from practical experience at both Qantas and Woolworths, that if you can win over the hearts and minds of staff, you can actually lift performance dramatically and consistently.

My first personal experience of the hearts and minds idea came from the Director of airports at Qantas. He was the first senior executive I knew who was actually prepared to talk about something other than a policy or procedure. He was prepared to talk about how people might feel. His thoughts were important to me in my early management years because it was the first hint or sign to me that there were senior managers in the company who understood there was a connection between how you treated people and what the performance outcome might be.

By his words and his actions, this particular Director treated people well and, for me, he moved the boundaries of what was possible. This created a space where it was okay to talk about people in a positive sense and to engage them in a shared vision that could influence the best possible outcome.

If you add this to the environment created by a modern and very caring CEO, then Qantas was in a great place at the time to be innovative and experiment with how to hit everyone's "hot button." We literally tried hundreds of initiatives, from providing all the statistical information about how the business was running, including KPI's and financial data, to ramping up communication and staff involvement in as many projects as possible. We also tried to get the frontline staff as close as possible to our customers at face-to-face forums that were often over a breakfast in a relaxed environment.

The most important recurring theme at the worksites I have been responsible for over 25 years was how much more effort people give when you treat them well and engage them in running the business. In every case the staff just wanted supervisors and managers to look them in the eye, say hello, and be interested in them and what they were doing.

This was and is very simple for those managers who like people but incredibly difficult for those managers who don't.

So, at Qantas and Woolworths over all those years, I watched people choose to give more every day and go that extra mile because they wanted to and once the momentum was created by a few it was hard for others not to participate. Everyone wanted to be part of what was happening. It was exciting and people liked being winners. Instead of sitting around bitching about how bad things were they knew that their job security was in their performance. This was understood and it was explicit.

When people look forward to coming to work, when they are having some fun, when they feel they can change what isn't working, they choose to give more every day. Engaged and treated well, staff at all sites lifted performance in every measure from customer service, safety, treating company property well, always doing the right thing and lowering operating costs by 15-25% (that's lowering unit costs, i.e. aircraft turnaround costs or how much it cost to pick a carton for a supermarket).

It didn't mean people ran around fast or worked in an unsafe manner but rather, they used their new found enthusiasm to come up with new ideas; they took ownership for their part of the business and found smarter and more productive ways of doing their jobs. When they identified a problem they also brought the solution to the table. Everyone came to work, absenteeism decreased. Safety performance in terms of medically treated injuries, as well as lost time injuries, decreased dramatically and once we showed we cared, it was amazing how staff started caring about one another and workplace injuries diminished.

Not to mention the complete disappearance of industrial action by unions. People were focused on the job. People were busy improving things. It was an exciting way to work and the 15-25% cost improvements just followed. There was a direct correlation between how people were treated and how they performed.

This happened for me in Qantas at Adelaide Airport, Perth Airport, Sydney Airport and in the Woolworths Distribution Centres across Australia.

Incredibly simple!

Grant: Poor Treatment Leads to High Absenteeism

Shane's continuous 25 year experience of treating people well and getting great returns from discretionary effort is contrasted with Perception Mapping research that shows treating people poorly leads to high levels of absenteeism. Withdrawing their labour is the main tool employees have to fight uncaring management. This withdrawal manifests in staff going slow, making purposeful mistakes or taking sickies. In Australia, taking a sickie is the most popular action.

Our research suggests that voluntary absenteeism is a good human indicator of total organisation performance and cultural harmony.

Quite simply, if your staff are not present, they can't perform. Not a lot of rocket science there but it has always amazed me that so many managers ignore the relationship and fail to see absenteeism or withdrawal of personal effort as the number one cultural indicator of potential performance.

Back in the Cluster days, some of Australia's best performing groups like National Rail, ICI Pharmaceuticals, CSR New Farm and Colgate-Palmolive all reported absenteeism rates around one percent while many of the poorer performers at the Clusters cited absenteeism rates of between five and eight percent. There were also government departments represented that were averaging between 10 and 12 percent.

This is all very concerning given the naturally occurring sickness rate in the Australian community is less than 1.8 percent, with much of that being attributed to older adults and young children who are not in the workforce. So, it is almost always true that organisations with greater than two or three percent absenteeism generally have major structural and cultural problems, with many managers who treat people poorly.

Over the years, our best practice tours visited a number of worksites with extremely low absenteeism rates. The Saturn Car Corporation, for example, reported absenteeism levels at 0.2 of one percent and all this with a policy of unlimited sick leave being available to all staff.

In fact, every organisation we have visited that operated without time clocks and with unlimited sick leave entitlements all said they experienced similarly low levels of absenteeism.

It's called caring and trusting and when people are trusted they never let you down.

Shane: Putting Time into Relationships

As Grant and I have emphasized throughout this story, taking time to have the coffee conversations, always treating people well and making a real effort to build the personal relationships will give you great performance returns.

You can't build relationships through emails or corporate memos. It takes time to get to know people and for them to get to know you. It takes time to just sit with staff and the unions, to listen and build a common language that all parties can use in a conversation that helps everyone understand what's important and what's possible. A common, positive language makes it easier for everyone to move in the same direction, instead of dealing with the manifestations of misinformation and emotion.

You must put in the time.

Building meaningful relationships is a lot harder than taking the traditional role of command and control, and meaningful relationships should be considered long term assets that can help steer the organisation through any challenges and save you millions of dollars along the journey.

It is too easy for you to walk into a room and tell staff what you think is important and then walk away feeling wonderful that now they all get what you're on about. What you didn't see as you walked away was everyone rolling their eyes and saying what a tosser.

I think telling is the easy way because it means you don't have to put any time into listening and building good working relationships.

It is so much harder to spend time getting to know everyone. In the many years of working with thousands of baggage handlers, customer service staff and pallet stackers in warehouses, I have spent thousands of hours meeting every possible person I could and I never met one who didn't want to be included in what we were doing; they all wanted to be part of the game. They wanted that good feeling of respect for what they did and to be able to go home at the end of the day and talk about it in a positive way.

The recurring theme through all of my work was building relationships. Over and over and over again going for a slow walk where people were doing the work, countless coffees and listening with real interest. Just getting to know them and for them, getting to know me.

Every day at Sydney airport I would start my day in the coffee shop and sure enough, there waiting for a chat, would be a manager, a couple of union delegates and some baggage handlers or customer service agents. Just imagine, nice coffee, a friendly chat, priority issues raised and resolved, talk about the future, how do we improve performance, respect all round and what a lovely way to start the day. And then, we were all ready to slip into the more formal part of the work.

My behaviour and actions were observed on a daily and hourly basis; it was talked about and judged by everyone. When problems or operational issues were raised we fixed them and moved on, with people doing the job included in the fixing. As people realised we would act on things they started to trust us as their leadership team.

This was all about building a relationship where we had to earn the trust of the workforce and the unions.

It takes time and thousands of small positive actions in management's daily behaviour to build a relationship where both parties are safe and comfortable so, that in both good and bad times, we can act as one. Quite a decisive and formidable team when all lined up together.

Building personal relationships with every staff member is critical to building a great team performance.

Grant: Managers Don't Listen

Shane is intuitively a good listener who likes people and will take the time to build the relationships but that's not a common trait amongst managers. In fact, data collected by Perception Mapping (PM), from hundreds of organisations, identifies managers 'not listening' as a seriously major irritation for frontline workers.

At PM, we always recommend organisations include some open text questions when conducting their staff surveys. The questions generally explore what the workforce thinks the organisation is doing well and where it could improve. These open questions provide much needed context to the quantitative responses. Not surprisingly, the more negative the quantitative responses, the more staff comment about their managers 'not listening'.

As Shane suggests, where managers don't take time to engage in consistent, meaningful conversations with staff, the data shows a fractured culture that invariably leads to poor performance.

Of course, this could all be easily fixed if managers had daily coffee conversations with staff but that's not how the story normally goes. More often than not, organisations attempt to resolve staff issues by moving to strengthen their performance appraisals and performance management systems. A behaviour that is dumb in the extreme when you consider the time and productivity costs and the loss of staff motivation.

Shane: What's Really Going On?

My time at Qantas was fantastic and the improvements we made at Sydney airport were terrific. It was the adventure of a lifetime but, eventually, it was time to move on.

A couple of years later, James Strong, who was now the Chairman of Woolworths, introduced me to Steve Bradley, the Chief Logistics Officer. Steve invited me to take on the role of National Operations Manager for all Woolworths Distribution Centres (DC's) across Australia, making me responsible for over 6000 staff.

Joining Woolworths in the retail supply chain environment was a big step. I grew up in the aviation industry and I knew it backwards. I knew absolutely nothing about retail or warehousing but the funny thing is, it never really bothered me not knowing the detail. When I didn't know what was being discussed or what was going on, I would simply say, I don't understand how that works can you explain it to me.

So here I was the National Operations Manager, Distribution Centres, Woolworths and right in the middle of another aggressive, defensive culture.

To begin, the running joke with the distribution centre managers was that "Shane wouldn't know the front end to the back end of a distribution centre." They were right.

All I could bring to the job was what I had learnt about people over 25 years and a basic knowledge of logistics. I needed to take a practical approach because the scale of the job was huge. Woolworths were building one of Australia's largest supply chains but it was falling apart from a people perspective.

In my first few months, I had two distribution centres withdraw their labour before evolving into fully-fledged strikes. Neither strike was about money, it was just a reaction by two workforces that did not like how they had been treated by management. There was high absenteeism, high worker injury, poor service to supermarkets and costs were haemorrhaging.

The disconnect between the company and its people was severe.

As an example, I started the job by visiting distribution centres, meeting the managers and walking around just talking casually with frontline staff I met along the way. I would always find time to go for a wander around the worksite alone, without managers and supervisors present. It was more relaxing and one thing I noticed early when walking the DC floors was that no one ever looked up from what they were doing. No one looked you in the eye. I also noticed there were a lot of broken boxes of stock lying around and it was often high value items like alcohol or shampoo. I would always ask the DC manager "do we have a problem with security or theft with all these open boxes lying around?"

On every occasion, the answer was a definite no!

This surprised me but they were adamant there was no problem with security or theft. Nevertheless, I pursued my hunch and one day I came across a manager who confirmed my thoughts. We had a chronic problem with theft. Stock was walking out the door but it just wasn't talked about. Nobody was having the crucial conversation.

Either management knew and didn't want to confront it or they didn't know what was going on in their own DC. Either way, it was not good. Millions of dollars were being stolen and written off as shrinkage and no one would discuss the problem.

When I raised the problem with the executive team, I was told to make sure that the security department knew and they would take care of it. No one got the connection between how people were feeling about the organisation and that the stealing behaviour was only one part of a culture that directly correlated to a high cost operation.

Other behaviours visible early on were, a lack of trust, poor communication, zero teamwork and everyone blaming the other person. All these signs were not good and I remember being a little nervous as I headed to my first quarterly review with the senior management group to present our performance over the previous three months.

There I was at the company board table with the CEO sitting directly opposite.

We started with all the pleasantries and then got down to business and the detail of the millions of unplanned dollars spent in logistics; it all became a bit tense. The CEO lent forward in his chair, with his eyes focusing in on me and said, in a no escaping way, "So Shane, you spent X millions of dollars at our distribution centre at Minchinbury, where did it go?"

At this point I must have looked like a rabbit in a spot light.

Well I didn't have a clue. Getting accurate information from my managers was proving incredibly difficult, they were all so busy fixing yesterday's problems, no one had time to plan for the future or be able to set a target and actually get there.

I only had one option and that was to tell the CEO exactly what I thought.

I put my hands forward in a cupped position to signify a bucket. I blurted out that I thought the millions of dollars in overspend were in two buckets. In one bucket is half the overspend and that was in the non-performance of every individual working in our supply chain.

He kept staring at me!

I went on, and the second bucket is the overspend on workers compensation for injured workers.

At this point he lent even further forward and said, "What do you mean, go on?"

I told him that whilst I could not find any records, it appeared on early calculations (and we had only just started compiling a list for each centre) we could have more than 250 people on some form of workers compensation payments and these people had to be replaced by other workers from a casual pool that was not in the budget.

This certainly got a reaction. The CEO asked for confirmation if this could be possible from the Chief Logistics officer who was present. He confirmed that it was. The meeting was then shut down and discussions were held later.

By the time we finished the review of workers compensation, we discovered we had 528 people injured who were neither being rehabilitated or moved to other jobs.

So here we were, scratching around like chooks in a barn yard, looking for small cost savings and right under our nose was almost an entire workforce for a distribution centre on some form of other duties or staying at home.

Woolworths is a fantastic company, highly successful, loves its people and is a real Australian icon. The company's determination to always do the right thing is unequalled. In the end the resources and effort that went into rectifying the situation was equal or more than the problem and it was eventually solved.

Yet the gap was there, what the company thought was going on with theft and injured workers and what was really happening were two completely different things.

The CEO later gave me the brief that when it came to rehabilitation or moving people into other jobs or out of the company, he would prefer we made five mistakes rather than put one person out on the street and out of work. He raised the bar incredibly high and we were true to his wishes.

But still the lesson was clear; managers have to know their staff and what's really going on in their company. Neither the theft nor the unmanaged injuries would have been an issue if previous management was having regular conversations and engaging with the staff.

Grant: The Best CEOs

My question to Shane when he told me the bucket story was to ask why the CEO didn't already know about the problem. Clearly the Chief Logistics officer knew and met with the CEO regularly. Why wasn't it discussed before? Why wasn't the CEO more out and about picking up the signs?

I have spent some time over the years studying the sustainable high performance of Southwest Airlines and their former CEO, Herb Kelleher. Herb is regarded as one of the great CEOs of the past 50 years and has always demonstrated a great love for the staff at Southwest. His relationship building and partying with his workforce is legendary.

From my perspective, Shane is very much like Herb and I have no doubt that had Shane become the CEO of a large company then that business would have enjoyed similar success to Southwest.

Southwest has a uniquely successful corporate culture that Harvard University and most other management training institutions insist their students study. This is understandable when we consider Southwest has been a best performer for over 40 years. When measured against their competitors over that period, Southwest has ranked number one for most of those years in customer satisfaction, baggage handling and on-time performance, plus they are best in class for profits as a percentage of revenues and assets and number one for continuous share growth value.

Over the years, I have invited Rita Bailey, a retired 35-year veteran employee at Southwest to talk with Australian audiences about the main factors in Southwest's phenomenal success. Every time she speaks, the audiences always ask her how Southwest has built such a loyal culture of people committed to best performance and how the company has delivered such consistent growth, profits and service in such a risky business.

Her answers have always been consistent. Southwest is fiscally disciplined, maintains a strong balance sheet, always watches costs and plans in the good times for the bad times.

She also suggests success for Southwest comes from staff being mandated to have fun at work. Where most businesses are impersonal, Southwest is like a family. So they don't hire bland, humourless people and that's what makes the difference. People who take themselves too seriously can kill a business and drive customers away.

Southwest doesn't want obedience; rather they look for people who perform on their own initiative. The organisation gives people the freedom to be themselves and run the business.

Rita has often quoted Herb Kelleher as saying, "If you create an environment where people can really participate then you don't need control. The people know what needs to be done, and they do it." This means greater discretionary effort, a volunteer mindset and less need for bureaucratic controls.

Moreover, Southwest ensure their leaders, including the CEO, are not preoccupied with little things like offices and titles. They demand their leader's do their people work first and their paper work second. They want them to be trouble-shooters, helpers. They want leaders to serve their staff and believe a genuine interest in people builds trust.

The company is strong on storytelling to keep the culture going through the generations. The stories of the battles and the way everyone chipped in to meet their challenges. They also provide variety by having people swap jobs for a day or more. Even pilots spend time working as check-in agents. It is one of the best tools for building understanding and teamwork.

Southwest now has a number of tough competitors who are executing well but the airline continues to grow because of its spirit and its commitment to the best customer experience. In essence, Southwest has always seen itself as a customer service organisation that flies airplanes rather than an airline that has customers.

Shane: Sharing the Stage

Very early on with Woolworths, I often had the feeling that head office seemed to spend all their time making sure we had policies and procedures to trap people doing the wrong thing. Workers were always viewed as causing problems; they went on strike, were often absent, they stole, their costs were too high and, according to head office, staff not only caused the problems, they were the problem.

And yet, as I had coffee conversations with staff in the DC's, I heard a very different view. I found they had a deep affection for Woolworths but a real unhappiness with management. The company and the distribution staff were obviously poles apart.

So, to get a better understanding of the situation inside the distribution centres, we took a group of frontline workers, supervisors, managers and a couple of executives offsite one evening to explore what the environment inside a DC was like and to understand just how the staff working their felt about their work, their DC and the company.

One interesting reaction from senior management was "what if they tell us about things we can't fix?"

This mindset was a real hurdle for management to get over. Could it be possible that rather than put all the issues on the table, in an open environment, managers preferred to have some issues they didn't know about? Maybe that's why they didn't know the extent of staff theft or how many people were away injured.

We started with about six frontline staff (people who picked and packed boxes, drove forklifts and general warehouse duties) and four managers or supervisors on each table and were very explicit about this being an open environment where people should feel safe to say what they think about how we were doing. Nothing was out of bounds and particular mention was made for managers not to be defensive about what they heard. We wanted to hear everything.

It was a great night, good discussions, very relaxed environment, everyone looked for the opportunity to contribute and I am sure everyone left with good feelings and intentions to share the discussions with their mates back at work.

We had asked the managers and supervisors to take their own notes during the session for a discussion to wrap up the evening. We also gave a commitment to staff that we would give them written feedback on their concerns and opportunities.

The list of what we could do better was long but what really surprised me, and the managers present, was that every table, without exception, had the same top three issues. Ten tables of people and they all listed the same top three things to change.

1. Everyone wanted their supervisor or manager to look them in the eye and say hello. They felt like they weren't

recognised or acknowledged as being people who actually worked there. Management would walk past them and ignore them.

2. Everyone wanted decent equipment to work with. It was frustrating for staff to start work and have no forklifts available, for example.

3. They all wanted a clean worksite. They said it was dirty and they were not proud of working in a mess. They even said if we supplied the brooms they would do the sweeping.

The list was long but on every table the theme or message was the same. People wanted to be involved in lifting performance and they wanted to be treated well. The message was consistent and simple; recognise me, treat me well, let's have a clean work site and some decent equipment and productivity will increase, and it did. Surprise, surprise!

What did I learn from this exercise?

It was important to have executives and managers in the room with the frontline. If I had just told the senior people the result of the session they probably would not have believed me, let alone feel they had a role in fixing the problems.

The session had been so successful that we decided to organise a similar but larger group to workshop what needed to be done and get larger buy in by everyone. We listed ideas, used hard data available on our performance and financial costs then created teams for implementation and agreed on responsibilities and accountabilities and time lines for delivery.

This was another positive experience, with everyone wanting to be part of what we were doing. We kept it simple with the goal being to treat people well and get a better performance outcome.

So well was it all going that we decided to present the ideas, goals and ambitions of the DC staff to the executives and management at the annual company conference, which was attended by 5000 staff from across the company. The conference was where each division reviewed past performance and forecast the future, including new products. It was very much a marketing/sales get together.

In fact, no frontline workers from logistics had ever been to a company conference let alone presented at one. We took about 25 staff from the Minchinbury DC to present what they had been working on. Their audience consisted of about 400 managers and supervisors from across the whole of logistics. The staff presenting were pickers, packers and forklift drivers. They were nervous but they knew what they were talking about and felt supported.

We were at the Sydney entertainment centre and DC staff were about to go on show. The stage was setup like a panel on a TV talk show and having the company chairman in the audience added a touch of extra nervousness.

Funnily enough, I didn't feel on edge at all or exposed to things going wrong. The staff knew their stuff and I knew the chairman, so it was actually a very safe, comfortable place to be. James was a real people person. I had watched him many times before do what I was trying to do.

Our staff came on stage and one by one they presented what they had work-shopped and where they had been making progress. Their lists of changes were extensive, with everyone taking responsibility and happy to be accountable. They were talking about how we could improve. This was a golden moment.

When they finished talking, the changes needed at the DC were evident to everyone in the room. I approached the microphone and told the audience that when I took the job, the chairman and executives described how they wanted the distribution centres to look, sound and feel. I then told the audience of managers and supervisors that what the executive wanted matched exactly what the DC staff on stage had just described as their vision, how they wanted their DC to look like and feel. The people doing the job had just articulated all the changes necessary to deliver on the company's objectives.

So I asked the audience "if this is what the chairman and executives want" and then pointing directly to our front line staff "and if this is what our staff want," then what's in-between, who is in the middle, who can make this happen?

And of course the very people who could drive this change, the supervisors, the middle managers and other people in-between were all sitting in the audience.

If I could have lived in that moment for weeks I would have stayed there but unfortunately I was on a stage with time running out. But I did hold the moment for just a while and everything was quiet until one of the supervisors in the audience stood up. He was emotional, he said I know these people on the stage, I know they can do it, he talked about how proud he was of them. Then more people in the audience took it in turns to contribute in the most positive of ways about how they could help and how he or she could do something to facilitate the changes in a very practical way.

There was also that extra warm feeling of the knowledge that there was a direct correlation between the improving behaviour of the group and our ever-decreasing costs of production.

Apart from all the good things happening in this moment, the personal pleasure I felt from having James Strong in the room while all this was happening was immense. I had observed how he went about business for more than 20 years, so I was happy for him to see what he always taught, "treat people with respect and treat them well and they will respond well."

At the end of the day we all packed up and went out for a celebration dinner. The chatter going on at the DC the next day was so positive it generated an immediate lift in performance.

Part of the positive feeling came from staff taking ownership of the problems but much of it came from the feeling people get when they can share the stage with management and have their ideas embraced.

Grant: Changing the Memetic Pattern

One of Shane's many redeeming characteristics is his ability as a manager to not only share the stage with staff but to give them leading roles. He is very good at giving staff an opportunity to change the conversation pattern by moving the clandestine blame conversations from the dark recesses of building corridors to solution conversations on a stage for the world to witness.

In essence, he is very good at changing the whole workplace culture by changing the memetic pattern. Every culture, be it family, work or societal, is driven in behaviour terms by its memes, with a meme being a self-replicating thought or idea.

If employees in a workplace keep reinforcing negative memes through their conversations then that workplace will have a negative work culture. Conversely, positive memetic patterns dominating the millions of conversations around a workplace will produce a positive work culture that can solve problems quickly and deliver outstanding results regularly.

Quite simply, what 30 years of cultural research has shown me very clearly is that large and complex culture change programs are a waste of time and money when culture change is much more easily gained by changing the memetic pattern.

Shane: The Cost Conversation and Who Leads the Fix

I really like being able to demonstrate and discuss the relationship between behaviour and costs in a practical, simple and uncomplicated way. Whether that's in unit costs of picking boxes or turning around airplanes, being able to look at the costs in a simple way is really important. In my experience, the power of frontline workers having this information daily transforms the way they think about their jobs.

Staff having all the cost information inevitably supports the conversation about them, and not management, being responsible for their job security. I have never accepted the position that I'm responsible for staff job security. I am here to help, I am here to provide information, I am here to make sure we have a strategy for success for our staff, our customers and our shareholders but staff job security is in their hands. They need to turn airplanes around or pick boxes at or below the market rate and provide great customer service to secure their employment.

Like all leaders, I have a used by date but if you want to be a baggage handler, check-in agent or picker packer for 20-30 years, then you had better make sure that what you are doing is affordable to the company. I prefer to employ my own staff to do the job rather than contract work out but it must be at or below the market rate. This is not a brutal or offensive statement; it is just an economic reality that we can't always protect higher costs. It's not always about base pay and conditions but also about what you do with what you've got.

Without exception, in my experience, once this reality becomes part of the memetic pattern then the whole pace picks up about winning and being successful. And this is where it gets exciting. In surfing terms this is where you catch a wave.

For example, when the purpose built Woolworths distribution centre in Brisbane, Queensland, opened, it was one of the biggest and last of the new centres to come online. It represented about 25 percent as a measure of cartons handled by Woolworth's supermarkets. In any measure it was massive in size, cost and workforce. It was one of the largest distribution centres in the world. Half automated, magnificent technology, just the bees knees of what's possible.

When the first day of operation arrived, it was filled with stock, 1000 people turned up for work, with great expectations and we fell flat on our face. We couldn't get new stock put away, we were unable to co-ordinate picking and we had difficulties staging deliveries. The technological interface between people and the IT systems was horrendous.

Sometimes, on starting new work sites, these problems happen but never on a scale like this. Our customers, the supermarkets, were screaming (mostly obscenities).

What we did have on site was an innovative leader and a team of doers who wanted to succeed. The team worked through the thousands of issues, one by one, until we were getting stock out the door. The tension was high but, as a group, they had all the information and the managers listened to the frontline staff who were able to offer all the fixes.

Our business case target to ensure the return on capital invested to build the new DC was 43.7 cents per carton picked (as published on the internet). On go live we were over 60 cents per carton. Multiply the difference by two million cartons per week, multiplied by 52 weeks and you can understand our potential over spend.

The reason I tell this story is because I was privileged to witness what it's like when staff choose to mobilise like a military campaign and stare down the enemy. The non-functioning issues were not of their making yet they stepped up as a team and attacked the problems with a wave of solutions. The situation we found ourselves in was a real risk to the company's wellbeing.

Over many meetings, many conversations, everyone knew we had to fix the problems and get to an operating figure of 43.7 cents. Everyone engaged their thoughts and actions on how to get there. Everyone was leading in their own field.

You could feel the passion and urgency in everyone and slowly they were bringing the costs down. With the last 13 cents to go, they all agreed to find one cent per week and reach the 43.7 cent target in 13 weeks. They hit the 43.7 cents per carton target in the thirteenth week.

I told the Brisbane team that they had left me in the very privileged position of sitting with the CEO and the senior management group and reporting the DC team's solid results of achieving the desired business outcome while redeeming our position with our customers. I thanked them sincerely and we celebrated the accomplishment achieved by the whole DC team.

It was an amazing experience and showed what an empowered group could achieve as long as managers stopped directing and allowed the workers to lead.

Grant: No One's in Charge

What Shane experienced in the Brisbane DC was real teamwork with everyone taking leadership roles to fix problems where they appeared.

Probably my greatest observation as a student of workplaces is that they work best when people are given the opportunity and responsibility to manage their own issues and to use teamwork to solve problems. Yet, most organisations are structured with too many managers thinking they need to take charge.

As we've discussed through this book, people can have titles of manager, supervisor, team leader, leading hand and so on but disengaged staff have a free will that allows them to take any order and manipulate the speed, quality and outcome any way they like.

Of course, when staff do this, take charge leaders don't like the outcome, so to take more charge, they put in place performance appraisals, performance management systems, pay for performance, infinite performance measures, performance reports and a myriad of other ways to catch people out, which further disengages and demotivates a staff group that could be giving 43.7 cents per carton returns if only no one was trying to take so much charge.

This is quite sad when you consider a regular coffee conversation and a little engagement will deliver everything the organisation needs.

Remember, the next time you're thinking, shall I invite everyone for coffee or just give them an order, choose coffee because they don't care for you, your order or anything that takes away their freedom.

Former Assistant Secretary of State in the Kennedy Administration, Harlan Cleveland, was an incisive student of leadership at both a political and corporate level. I listened to him speak at a number of conferences through the eighties and nineties and remember him arguing that in his observation and experience, "people know by instinct that, in a pluralistic democracy, no one is, can be, or is even supposed to be in control. By constitutional design reinforced by the information rich environment, we live in a nobody-in-charge society."

He continued that "if the question is important enough, people-in-general get to the answer first. Then the experts and pundits and pollsters and labour leaders and lawyers and doctors and business executives and foundation officers and judges and professors and public executives, many of them afflicted with hardening of the categories, catch up in jerky, arthritic moves with all deliberate speed."

At a macro level, Cleveland identified that the movements for women's rights, protection of the environment, civil rights, energy conservation and a host of other changes have "boiled up from the people." "They were not," he argues, "generated by the established leaders in government, business, labour, religion or higher education."

This people power is exactly what we see in workplaces. Where the ideas of staff are valued and they are engaged in driving the performance outcomes, they always perform well. Where some arthritic leader tries to control their every move, the performance suffers.

The reality is, people hate authority.

In fact, according to research by Manz and Sims, quoted in *Business Without Bosses*, the "baby boomers have a set of life and work values that are very different from that of their parents and grandparents. Most of all, they are less tolerant of bosses. They also have lower overall job satisfaction and less desire to lead or manage, move up the organizational hierarchy or defer to authority."

To complicate matters further for traditional management, Manz and Sims suggest the newer generations are even "slower to commit and less loyal to organisations" It's also true that organisations are less loyal to their workers. Moreover, younger people "don't bow to any authority. Younger workers will not respect you just because you're the boss. They want to know why they are being asked to do things. They question authority and they have a disregard for hierarchies."

Younger people are generally better educated, competitive and want opportunities to learn and have fun at work.

Of course, this dislike of authority figures presents a new challenge for managers, who duly trundle off looking for the next best thing in management training to help them manage the great unwashed. This behaviour is a common response to staff misbehaving and has been going on forever in organisations.

Peter Block, who wrote a great leadership book called *Stewardship*, suggests all modern leadership training teaches manages 'how to control workers," albeit, in often very subtle ways.

Sadly, too many managers are always on the lookout for the next quick way to solve their people problems. Very few will ever take the time, like Shane, to have the coffee conversations.

When Professor Michael Magill wrote *American Business and the Quick Fix*, he described how most companies have been on an endless merry-go-round, chasing quick fix management techniques to cure everything that ails their organisations.

Magill suggests that "management by walking around, management by objectives, excellence management, one minute management, quality management" and many other expert approaches are fundamentally flawed because they all possess an element of "doing it to" the workers.

No quick fix management technique has the slightest hope of optimising organisational performance if management still holds the control and power over staff.

There you have it. You're not in charge, nobody likes you and the quick fixes won't work. So, it is probably time to try the only thing we have seen consistently work, regular coffee conversations and letting staff have a go at self-managing.

Shane: Three Percent of Anything

Spending time in many coffee conversations with staff at Sydney airport helped me appreciate the thousands of decisions they were making every day to help the business perform. This is in contrast to a common perception many managers have that people just attend work, complete their tasks and go home without ever having to think.

Having discussions with the aircraft cleaners, for example, highlighted how they made seemingly minor decisions about how they would place a pillow on a seat or cross the seat belts to make sure the seat was presented for the aircraft to look new for every single customer.

Respecting the detail of those decisions helped everyone understand it was the culmination of thousands of thoughts and actions, by everyone, that determined if planes departed on time, what level of customer service was delivered, where we were on that performance continuum and, ultimately, the costs of operating.

Staff loved talking about the detail and importance of what they were doing. Somehow, respecting all these thousands of small decisions people were making every day made them feel valued, so when the detail of how to save one minute of time or the detail of that pillow being placed just perfectly was appreciated by management, it made it possible for people to feel good about owning the whole job.

I have heard it said that "when people work like they are all singing from the same sheet of music, it sounds great." Well that's what it was like at Sydney airport, it sounded great.

And it was all about that pillow.

Fast forward a few years and here I was walking through a very large distribution centre, with a senior executive, looking around and chatting about how things were going. We talked with staff, checked out some new equipment and had a nice day all round but as we were walking past a guy stacking a pallet of boxes for a supermarket delivery, the executive quietly whispered to me, "what a shit job, we cannot make that interesting."

I nearly fell over! That "shit job" was costing about $40,000 a year, it was a real person doing it and we will probably have a relationship with this person for 20-30 years. After 20-30 years, he will probably have a sore back and we have 5000 more people doing the same job just like this guy. I couldn't believe we could have 5000 shit, uninteresting jobs.

Now let's have a look at that "shit job" another way.

This guy is about to stack a pallet, with boxes all different sizes and shapes. He chooses the first box to go somewhere on the pallet and how he does that determines where the next box will go, he does this over and over again and if he makes really good choices about how to stack that pallet, he may get 70 boxes on that pallet. If he chooses really well he may get 71 or 72 boxes loaded on the pallet.

In our business model we may plan for 70 boxes to be loaded on every pallet and if we achieve this we make budget. However, if we only get 68 boxes we will blow our budget with extra pallet hire and transport costs. But the real kick is this, if every person stacks 71 or 72 boxes on 50,000 pallets a week we literally save millions of dollars a year that goes straight to the bottom line.

Let's express it another way, if we get one extra box on every pallet we save 1.5 percent off the transport cost. Two boxes on every pallet saves three percent off costs.

Consider less pallet hire, less pallets to move in the warehouse and less transport costs. All because we value that guy stacking pallets and what he is thinking about.

Three percent is a lot.

And what I would really like to do is have a chat with this guy about what I can do to make his life a little easier. How can we help to save his back?

Funny thing, there were many things we could do to help and that's my role as a leader, to listen and help. That's how I best influence high performance outcomes.

Grant: Have the Tough Conversations Well

Maybe it's because the memetic pattern of 'shit job' type conversations have dominated organisations for such a long time that safety violations, stealing and other problematic behaviours are so common?

When talking with Shane about these behaviours, I wasn't surprised to hear that senior Woolworths managers were unaware of similar problems in their DC's because managers being out of touch or turning a blind eye to poor behaviours is a regular complaint in Perception Mapping surveys.

More specifically, it is common in organisations for most staff to avoid the tough conversations. Thirty years of research by the VitalSmarts group has identified that the tough conversations in organisations are rarely managed well. They show clearly that many people lack the crucial conversation skills necessary to ensure everyone wins when the stakes are high, views are opposing and emotions run strong.

Shane is one person with a natural flair for handling the tough conversations well because he spends so much time in conversations with so many different people. He has had thousands of hours of practice and it's that practice, just like the hours of technical practice needed to be a top performer in any field, which makes the difference.

In fact, in my 30 years working with managers, except for Shane, I have never seen anyone make enough time to deliberately practice the conversation skills required to engage everyone and solve all problems.

Malcolm Gladwell, in *Outliners: The Story of Success*, listed 10,000 hours of practice, as the level of practice that accounted for genius. Gladwell suggests ten thousand hours of practice was how the Beatles got so good. Other British scientists have also produced studies confirming the ten thousand hour threshold for greatness, based on studies of musicians, sportsmen and chess players.

Shane has invested more than 10,000 hours in developing his coffee conversation skills, so his success is no surprise. The question for most managers, however, is where do I start? The answer is to start with at least one hour of coffee conversations every day, then build up to two and three hours a day and in 15 years, you will be brilliant.

Shane: Successful Managers Really Like People

As I mentioned previously, from my experience, extra discretionary effort is created when work is a fun place and staff look forward to coming each day. Discretionary effort occurs where people are having fun, where they feel trusted, where they own their job, have the freedom to think about what needs to be done and can get on with doing it. It's where people are prepared to have a go, take a chance and always feel supported.

This is where the really good stuff happens. It's where great teamwork abounds and where everyone knows their responsibilities and enjoys being accountable for their own performance. The bigger the challenge the more people get excited and are creative about how to get there.

To support this effort, management need to be technically capable but more importantly, they need to like people.

I like to select my direct reporting managers and create an empowering, supportive environment for them. And in turn, I like them to select their own teams and create a similar environment. I've always found that if I select well and my managers enjoy how we work together, they have no trouble doing the same with their staff.

Woolworths had built a magnificent new supply chain and had a great group of technical managers and administrators running it. They were an excellent group of logistics specialist but mostly void of the people management qualities required to lead very large worksites of up to 1000 people.

Sometimes, early on, it appeared staff were being treated like the boxes they were handling. If a worker got injured a manager would just pick up the phone and call for a replacement through a casual employment agency. It was known as the "disposable worker".

So to help improve the situation we started selecting leaders who actually cared about people to manage these super-sized sites. We wanted managers who would stop and talk and listen, people who could balance the technical side of the business with the human side. I remember one manager commenting at the time "so we aren't in the business of moving boxes any more, we're in the people business." I took that as a sign we might be making some progress. Woolworths employed over 6000 staff across all the DC's, so someone had to care about them.

To begin, we selected some managers from outside the organisation who had demonstrated these characteristics in previous roles. Then we looked a few levels below the normal management levels inside the DC's and what we found was really interesting.

A group of relatively young leaders who technically new the business very well but who also had the social qualities. They were still fresh and had not been exposed to the bullyboy attitude of management. They cared about people they worked with, had passion and energy for the job and were very keen to demonstrate what they could do. They were really hungry for the opportunity and, most importantly, they liked having fun.

I was once asked by a senior executive to interview a guy who was interested in a career as a manager in a DC. I read his resume and it was very impressive. He had all the logistic qualifications, had a military background and, on paper, appeared perfect. I arranged to meet him at a DC and thought, rather than a normal interview process, we would go for a walk on the floor of the distribution centre and let him meet people.

On meeting him at the DC it was clear from the outset that he matched his CV; fit, healthy and presentation perfect, all the boxes ticked. So off we went for our tour and it was interesting, as I introduced him to a range of staff, I saw no signs or signals from him that he was actually engaged or interested in the people. He displayed no eye contact nor did he ask any questions about what they were doing. I saw no signs at all, so I asked him 'how can I tell if you like people?' He said, "I do not know how to answer that." I was really looking for someone who could interact, enjoy the conversation with people doing the work. I am sure this guy is very good at what he does but I really needed someone who could connect with people.

Grant: Attitude is Everything

It's not just managers who need to have a positive attitude towards other people, it's everyone. Unequivocally the most common saying heard at every high performance site visit is "hire for attitude and train for skills."

Hire the wrong person, with the wrong attitude and all the training and coaching in the world is not going to help.

Shane and Grant: Where to from Here

That's the end of the stories and conversations for now. We hope they have given you some understanding of the Coffee Conversation approach to creating high performance workplace cultures.

As we mentioned in the beginning, every workplace culture is developed through millions of random conversations that form a memetic pattern over time and create the cultural narrative that drives everyone's behaviour. Change this memetic pattern and you will change the culture.

The best place to start the change process is with Coffee Conversations.

If you would like to learn more about Coffee Conversations, please feel free to visit us at www.coffeeconversations.com.au.

Made in the USA
Charleston, SC
16 November 2012